£8

THE ALTERNATIVE
SHOPPING GUIDE

EASTERN COUNTIES

Barbara Cameron

STABLE
PUBLISHING
COMPANY

First published in 1994
by The Stable Publishing Company
Woolsthorpe by Belvoir
Grantham
Lincolnshire

Designed and produced by the Pen & Ink Book Company Ltd,
Huntingdon, Cambridgeshire.

Cover photograph by Roger Mockford, Commercial Photographer
(☎ 0636 71942)

Printed in England

CONTENTS

INTRODUCTION

This book is designed for those of you who appreciate quality and value in your shopping, or buying something that is a bit different, and those who secretly (or otherwise) hate shopping. By using it you can appreciate our lovely countryside and have a good day out, exploring it, and shopping at the same time.

How many of us have found a super little shop whilst on holiday, intended to go back sometime, and promptly forgotten where it was located? It can be a chore struggling into towns and cities, heavily congested with traffic, and expensive to park. Out of town shopping centres tend to have a certain uniformity about them and you still have to carry your purchases back to the car park.

This book gives a whole new meaning to Out-of-Town shopping, which is gentler, friendlier and much more enjoyable. Neither does it cost you extra. All the businesses in the book have been selected for quality, value, 'something different', or are in totally unexpected locations. The double page area map and the individual location maps should ensure they are easily found and the photographs give you some idea of what to expect.

You can now combine a great day out with a shopping trip, personal service and free parking. You may travel a little further and we suggest you do part of your journey on the major road and then branch off. It is very enjoyable, with less hassle and a great range of quality goods at reasonable prices. With a bit of luck you can save the cost of a good lunch, or spend the savings on some other little luxury. You will have found places you didn't know existed, and some you had forgotten. If, like me, you have friends and family scattered all over the country, look at the map and you may find a small detour on your next visit, which will enable you to take them 'something different'. The same maxim applies if your work involves travelling – allow a little extra time to shop. I have found many places just by taking the scenic route instead of the motorway. The problem is usually seeing a hanging sign too late to brake and turn in.

Motorways and major roads are great for getting from A to B, and the by-passes around our small towns and villages ensure the safety of their inhabitants – but what a lot we miss by not stopping to explore! Many exciting businesses are to be found tucked away in side streets of small towns, in small villages and way out in the countryside in farm barns, converted stables and the old coach houses of stately homes. Very often the goods for sale are produced on the premises and thus sold direct to the public at a saving. If not, the overheads are usually lower and consequently so are the prices. If neither is the case the products are usually individual in some other way, as is the setting, so your journey is still worthwhile.

Most of the businesses we have included are open all year round, one or two closing during January and February, but unless the weather is particularly bad you can still appreciate the countryside and the quieter roads. Consider a walk by the sea in winter, appropriately dressed, preceded by present shopping for Christmas and the purchase of fresh farm foods for the table! You arrive home refreshed and relaxed.

The thing to do on one of these expeditions, no matter what time of year, is to go prepared, but with an open mind. Make a list in the back of the book of the things you need, or what you need them for, make a note of sizes or colours that require matching – better still take fabric samples with you. Go intending to buy if you find something suitable, so take your cheque book! It is almost 'impulse' buying, but a bit of planning before hand means you are less likely to make mistakes, or have to make a return trip because you forgot to take measurements. You will however, probably make return trips for other purchases, tempted by the old fashioned service and the choice of quality merchandise.

Put an empty cardboard box and an old towel in the boot of the car and a cool-box – now you can buy breakable objects and know they will still be in one piece after travelling; or ice-cream and know it will still be ice-cream when you get it home! I once picked pounds and pounds of raspberries in Sussex only to find they had fermented with the heat when I arrived home the following day – a total waste of time and money, and – no cool-box!

If the opening times given are not too specific or by appointment only, do please telephone first.

Friends who have had the 'tip-off' to some of the places in this book have been amazed at their 'finds', you will be too. Have some great days shopping, keep the book in the car, and please mention it when making purchases.

THE EASTERN COUNTIES
An introduction to some of the attractions

England is a north to south country. Most of us have 'passed through' or reply 'I've heard of it' when we get a query on this area. And yet we should not, for these counties hold within their boundaries some of the most beautiful scenery, many of the most atmospheric sites, and some of the most exciting places to discover in the whole of England. Rutland Water, Sherwood Forest, the Norfolk Broads, Constable Country – all names to conjure with and places we all say 'We must go there sometime'. The Alternative Shopping Guide is a means of discovering attractive places combined with a practical shopping expedition. To enjoy shopping is our aim, and this section of the book offers some suggestions on the attractions of the region.

Where do we mean by 'The Eastern Counties'? This guide covers Lincolnshire (south), Nottinghamshire (east), Leicestershire (east), Cambridgeshire, Norfolk, Suffolk and Essex (north). The area lies roughly either side of the A1, the Great North Road running south to north as the eastern artery of England. And what a beautiful area it is! In the north there is the famous Sherwood Forest with its wooded walks and intriguing legends, bordered on the east by the rolling wolds of north Lincolnshire. South Lincolnshire has a fascination all its own with its vast skies and great fields of bulbs and flowers. The silent Brecklands and shimmering Broads sweep across Norfolk in the middle of the region, and to the south it tapers out into the quiet red brick and timbered villages of Suffolk and Essex. And, of course, there is the sea right along the length of this region, with a mixture of long empty beaches and old fishing ports.

But it's not just the geography that distinguishes the Eastern Counties. There are also some of the grandest stately homes and elegant parklands in England – Blickling Hall, Felbrigg Hall and Holkham Hall in Norfolk, Burghley House and Grimsthorpe Castle in Lincolnshire, and Wimpole Hall in Cambridgeshire amongst others.

So often in England today our cities are monuments of inconvenience. Not so the small towns of Eastern England, with a few exceptions. You can still wander round Cromwellian Huntingdon, or follow the Middlemarch trail round Georgian Stamford, or walk the seafront in Southwold in comfort. Of course the great tourist cities of Cambridge and Norwich or

commercial Peterborough are as busy and congested as you would expect.

All in all, this is an area of great variety, great charm and delightful individuality. Here you can still combine travel and shopping in comfort.

A brief summary of some of the Places to Visit that you can combine with your shopping is suggested, district by district.

NOTTINGHAMSHIRE, LEICESTERSHIRE AND LINCOLNSHIRE

- **Sherwood Forest** – 450 acres of ancient oaks and silver birches in the Sherwood Forest Country Park at Edwinstowe in Nottinghamshire, with an informative Visitor Centre, exhibitions about Robin Hood, many special events (especially for children), a restaurant and large car park. Admission – Free, but parking fee of £1.

- **Holme Pierrepont National Water Sports Centre** – situated near Nottingham, this is the home of Olympic class rowing in England. It combines a country park with a 2000 metre watersports course – the whitewater slalom course is a thrill in itself. Admission – Free.

- **Retford, Southwell and Newark** – three Nottinghamshire towns of great age and interest. The Minster and the Saracen's Head Hotel (where Charles I, surrendered to Parliament) in Southwell are very special buildings, as is Newark Castle (where King John died). The market squares of Retford and old Newark (itself besieged three times in the Civil War) hold delightful street markets and are surrounded by fine old buildings. Retford of course is associated closely with the Pilgrim Fathers Story – it all began at Babworth and Scrooby villages near the town.

- **Rutland Water** – the biggest man-made reservoir in Europe, with long views over the water, fine walks – and cycle rides for the energetic, and all set in the rolling hills and pretty villages of the old county of Rutland, near Oakham.

- **Grantham, Stamford, Bourne and Boston**
  Grantham – Isaac Newton and Margaret Thatcher lived here, and the town not only has a 282 ft church spire, the very old Angel and Royal Hotel, but an inn with a living beehive outside it. Nearby is dramatic Belvoir Castle high on its peak over the Vale of Belvoir.
  Stamford – surely one of England's most beautiful towns, with its beautifully preserved Georgian town houses (the location for the TV series 'Middlemarch') and innumerable spines, and bounded on the south side by the grandeur of Elizabethan Burghley House and its park.
  Bourne and 'the Deepings' – small ancient towns of quiet charm set on the edge of lowlying Fenland, yet still having considerable areas of forest walks. Hereward the Wake, Saxon opponent of William the Conqueror, was born in Bourne, as was Charles Frederick Worth, the Paris fashion designer.
  Boston – the medieval port famous for its 'Stump', the tapering tower of St. Botolph's Church, and famous as the base for the Pilgrim Fathers before they fled to Holland. Near the town lie the flat, brooding shores of the Wash, world famous for its wildlife.

NORFOLK,, SUFFOLK AND ESSEX

- **North Norfolk Coast** – one of the greatest sites for 'twitchers' in Britain, and dotted with bird sanctuaries. This quiet protected coastline of winding lanes and flint stone

houses is unique. The little pockets of seaside villages and towns like Cley-next-the-Sea still have a flavour of a much earlier age. Natural rather than Man-made is still the attraction – sailing, bird watching, seal trips and walking on the shore watching the sea birds is what you go here for. The great Stately homes of Sandringham and Holkham Hall in the west of this area, and Blickling Hall and Felbrigg Hall in the east sit well in this quiet landscape, dotted with attractive old small towns like Downham Market and Nelson's 'The Burnhams'.

- **Breckland & Broadland** – two contrasting Norfolks. Breckland, 'the Kingdom of the rabbit', is still heathland and stabilising Forestry Commission conifers, but this ancient area was probably first cleaned by Neolithic man over 4000 years ago as Grime's Graves testifies. Around and across it, winding lanes and distant church towers make this a restful landscape. Broadland dominates Norfolk east of busy Norwich, as a centre of pilgrimage for water-loving 'landlubbers', while pilgrimages of a different sort have been made for centuries to the sacred places of Walsingham and Bury St. Edmunds. You can wander through delightful small towns like Regency Swaffham and Georgian Holt through quiet ancient villages on roads that lead inevitably to the long open sea shore, or stand on Polter Higham Bridge and watch the inexperienced 'captains' try to take their cruises through the tiny arches often with disastrous results!

- **Constable Country** – in Suffolk and Essex. In the north of this region you can still see the professional trawlermen in Lowestoft or walk the long beaches below the cliffs in Aldeburgh or Southwold, delightful towns with an old-world quietness about them. Strange oddities hide away in this area to surprise you – like the 'House in the Clouds' at Thorpeness near Aldeburgh or Black Shuck, the Black Dog of East Anglia, depicted on Bungay's town sign, or the 'Dutch Quarter' of Colchester, or the lighthouse soaring above the chimney pots in Southwold, or the archaeological 'digs' at Sutton Hoo. Flatford Mill, Long Melford and Lavenham look much as they did in Constable's day, and this area south and west of Ipswich is full of mellow timbered villages often brightly colour-washed, remainders of the once great medieval woollen and weaving industries here. It is easy to see what captivated the ever popular Constable (born in East Bergholt) and Gainsborough (born in Sudbury) in the south Suffolk and Essex landscape.

It is no wonder that one of the vast numbers of American airmen stationed in East Anglia found the Eastern Counties 'just as the story books back home said England was like'.

T.D. Phillips

ACKNOWLEDGEMENTS

Thank you to all the people who have helped in the production of this book. Especially to Roger Mockford (Photography) Ltd 0636 71942 for the front cover photograph. Smith-Woolleys, Chartered Surveyors for support and encouragement and to David, Sue and Richard, and Pam for putting up with me.

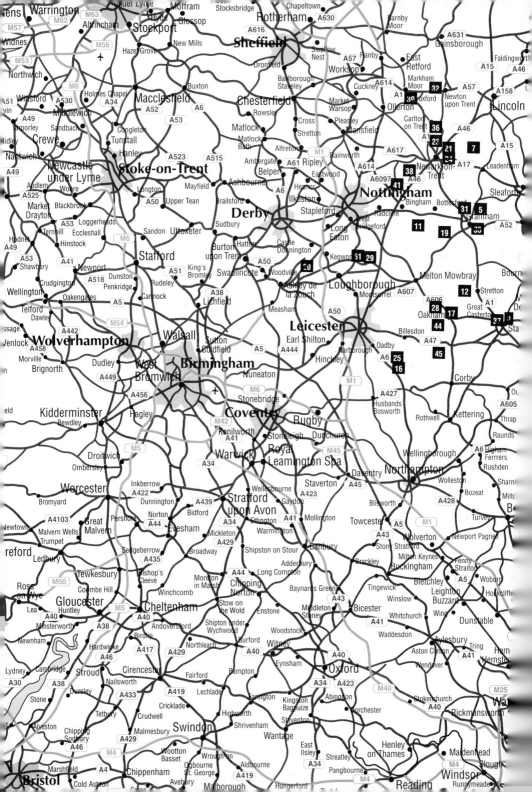

GREETHAM VALLEY GOLF CLUB

Greetham
Oakham
Rutland
LE15 7RG

☎ 0780 460666
Fax: 0572 812616

*Everything for the golfer.
Golf clubs and accessories,
clothing for golf and walking,
knitwear.*

Opening hours
Monday – Sunday 8 am – 9 pm

Parking adjacent to
clubhouse

Greetham Valley Golf Club has been developed
with the inside knowledge from golfers and the
expertise of landscape architects and civil engineers
to provide the perfect environment for the sport. It is
set in 200 acres, containing many mature trees, to
which 15,000 more trees and shrubs have been added.
Greetham Valley comprises of an 18-Hole
Championship Course (6,569 yards long) a 9-Hole par
3 floodlit course (1,460 yards long), and a 21 bay
floodlit driving range. Designed by golfers for golfers
everyone is welcome, including weekday societies
and Pay & Play – some memberships may be
available if you enquire.

The Pro Shop is extremely well stocked from all the
leading golf manufacturers. Amongst the clothing
you will find knitwear by Pringle and Glenmuir, golf-
suits which are waterproof and equally suitable and
attractive for walking, by Goretex and Proquip. The
shop is open to anyone and you are sure of a
welcome and advice if needed, whether buying for
yourself or a present for the golfer in your life.

The luxurious clubhouse incorporates the Lake
View Restaurant, which is also available for
conferences, weddings or other functions. The
atmosphere is relaxed and friendly but totally
professional. A great place to visit in a lovely setting
and close to the A1.

OAKHAM ORIENTAL RUGS

6 The Maltings
Mill Street
Oakham
Rutland
Leicestershire
LE15 6EA

☎ 0572 724441

*Hundreds of fine hand-knotted
rugs*

Opening hours
Monday – Saturday
10 – 5.30
Sunday 1 – 5

Free parking in Oakham

Tucked away in a small complex off Mill Street you can enter a world of dry desert winds, billowing nomad tents and glowing colours. Rugs of all shapes, sizes and colours, old and new, adorn the walls and sprawl in piles upon the floor. Rugs from Persia, China, Turkey, India, Afghanistan and many other countries have been carefully chosen to give you the best quality and the best value the owners can find. Nearly all the rugs are hand-knotted whether they are made of wool, silk or cotton and the range of patterns and colours is breathtaking. Although they are referred to as rugs the sizes and shapes vary from prayer mat to room size. Prices start around £20. The premises have been doubled in size to cater for an ever growing number of clients who come again and again. Rugs are an ideal way to add new life and colour to your home and you are welcome to try them in situ. They look equally good in old or modern settings.

If you wish to browse or look for ideas this is a place where you will feel comfortable and the owners are happy to answer your questions. The world at your feet!

THE TABLE PLACE LTD

The Table Place was founded in 1983 by Marietta King and Peter Baker, both cabinet makers, helped by a part-time wood machinist. Since then it has expanded and prospered, attracting an increasing number of discerning customers from the UK and overseas to its showrooms in Oakham, Rutland, Leicestershire. Many visitors are surprised and delighted to discover this 'Aladdin's Cave' of quality furniture.

The secret of success? No magic formula – simply consistent, reliable quality allied to an impressively wide range of designs. Attention to detail and customer service are further hallmarks of The Table Place, where the staff are always happy to discuss individual specifications, colour matching, or any other special requirements. They know what they are talking about, and it is a joy to buy furniture straight from craftsmen in a quality you can see and feel.

The furniture is hand-made and hand-finished in the company's own workshops. Mahogany pieces have the traditional warm brown glow, rich and inviting. Yewtree has a more mellow look, soft and relaxing. Oak and antique pine are newer additions to the range.

The Table Place in Fenstanton, serving Chambridge, Huntingdon and Bedford, is situated in a beautiful old house, where expressions such as "Isn't it lovely to see such quality", and "sensible prices" are heard.

50 Queens Walk, Stamford
PE9 2QE

☎ 0780 57994

Personally designed – Bridal wear, special occasion wear, casual wear

Opening hours
By appointment

Parking outside

Please telephone for
appointment
and directions

DESIGNER SEWING SKILLS

Julia Chamberlain is the highly talented proprietor of this business which she operates from a small workroom. She is well-known locally for the beautiful bridal and evening wear she creates so lovingly from her clients ideas and her own design expertise. When I visited she was working on a silk jacket for one client and a tailored fine wool and silk 3-piece suit for another. The prices are very reasonable, so if you have never had clothes made to measure before you will find that the prices compare very favourably with middle to up-market clothes shops.

Some of her clients are non-standard sizes but the majority are those who simply have difficulty finding their ideal garments elsewhere and having once experienced the choice of fabric and design come back again and again. Please allow some time before you need your wedding dress or special outfit, as unlike shop bought clothes you will need one or two fittings once you have decided on the design and fabric. It is, however, very exciting to have your own ideas translated into working designs and a finished garment.

STAMFORD ANTIQUES CENTRE

Exchange Hall, Broad St.,
Stamford, Lincs PE9 1PX

☎ 0780 62605

*A wide range of quality
antiques and collectables*

Opening hours
Monday – Saturday 10 – 5
Sunday 12 – 5
closed 1 week after
Christmas and 1 week after
Easter

Within 1 mile of the A1 is this Aladdin's cave of approximately 40 antique dealers operating in one centre in the beautiful 'Middlemarch' Georgian town of Stamford.

How do you summarise what such a centre has for sale? Some of the items are of course for the specialist collector – thimbles, snuff boxes, candlesticks, silver cutlery. But there will be some things that all of us would love in our own homes – Edwardian dressing tables, corner cupboards, mahogany dining tables and chairs, bookcases, coffee tables and other furniture. One of the biggest collections is of prints. You may, of course, be looking for something personal, like costume jewellery, or for a gift, like a piece of china or glass. After all, how much nicer does your wine taste poured from an antique decanter in crystal glasses which have not cost a fortune!

There is something quaintly fascinating too about a building which has 16th Century cellars and has to close one week each year for the Pantomime and another week for the Operatic Society to take place. And remember that over the Georgian houses you can see the elegance of Elizabethan Burghley House.

The

UPPINGHAM

Established 1966

DRESS AGENCY

2 – 6 Orange Street
Uppingham
Rutland
Leicestershire
LE15 9SQ

☎ 0572 823276

*Ladies wear, mens wear,
childrens wear, occasion wear,
new & used riding and
country wear*

Opening hours
Monday – Saturday 9 – 5.30
Sunday 12 – 4

Parking free in nearby
square or side street

UPPINGHAM DRESS AGENCY

This attractive double-fronted shop is larger than it looks. Since it was established in 1966 it has become one of the largest and best known dress agencies in the country. The building contains ten separate rooms each containing different types of quality clothing, for men, women and children of all ages. If you wish to sell your unwanted garments you are assured of discreet professional service and their extensive advertising, locally and nationally, should ensure you recoup some of your original outlay. However, you may well be tempted to spend it on the same premises as they stock top designer labels in ball gowns, occasion wear, dinner suits for gentlemen, casuals and separates.

Used riding and country wear is obtained from all over the country, in addition to new stocks of leading makes, giving you a large choice. Top names such as Drizabone, Toggi (wet and dry wax) Caldene, Eque-sport, Belstaff and Mr Fox are represented in outdoor garments and fleeces, for small children to adults. There is also a good selection of millinery and other accessories – a very economical way of dressing up for special occasions! The staff are helpful and friendly in this well organised shop and the proprietors are on hand if needed. Coffee is available and major credit cards are accepted.

T.P. ACTIVITY TOYS

T.P. Activity Toys have won awards for safety and 'real' play value. All their designs are made from quality materials and the best British Steel, which is galvanised for strength, to withstand tough treatment and to last.

The two working farms which have Activity Centres in this area hold a wide range of stock and your children can try them out before you buy in an outdoor situation. It is often found that children actually prefer a different item from the one you had in mind. Climbing frames can have sections added at a later date thus providing years of enjoyment without prohibitive cost. Most of the equipment is supplied flat-packed for storage and transport, but is easy to assemble following the clear instruction sheet. Both businesses will deliver free locally, and further afield by arrangement. Catalogues are available showing the full selection available, including trampolines, sand pits, tree toys, goal nets, an indoor creative play selection and accessories. Both farms also stock larger trampolines by 'Super Tramp' and Mrs. Bradley at Kidzbiz hires out bouncy castles and ball ponds for parties.

These are great places to visit when buying toys, and the prices are very competitive. 'For fitness and fun' would be an appropriate motto indeed.

Chandlers Farm Equipment
Sleaford/Lincoln Road
Belton
Grantham
Lincolnshire
NG32 2LX

☎ 0476 590077

*Kitchenware, hardware,
pet foods and accessories,
country clothing & footwear.
garden & DIY products*

Opening hours
Monday – Friday 8 – 5.30
Saturday 8 – 5
Sunday 10 – 4

Own car park

GREEN ACRES

Chandlers is a well known name in the area for farm equipment of all types, but in December 1993 they opened a new modern store adjacent to their car showroom. The store is light, airy and well planned stocking all the items you never quite knew where to buy. Items such as galvanised buckets and coal hods, door mats, tilley lamps and lengths of chain amongst them. Their clothing department includes wax jackets by Harry Hall at very reasonable prices, donkey jackets, quilted shirts, hats and caps, riding boots and sweaters. They have a good selection of body warmers and fleece jackets also, and the range is expanding. There are items for all the family and toys for the children. What small child could resist a pedal tractor which is a Massey Ferguson look-a-like? How many grandparents could deny them?

The gardening department has an excellent range of mowers and quality tools. There are fertilisers, weed killers, moss killers and patio cleaners – all very well displayed and sensibly priced. If you cannot find what you want – ASK. The staff are helpful, friendly and very knowledgeable and justifiably proud of this superb store. Whilst shopping for yourself remember the family pet. There is a full range of pet foods and accessories.

RUDKINS

An old school building in a side road in Grantham and a converted granary at Peakirk seem unlikely places to visit for quality furniture. However once you have entered, the range is incredible. Both buildings are large and full of character in their own right, which enhances the well organised displays of furniture. All the pine furniture is handwaxed on their own premises and the range is enormous – everything from wall and spice racks to double wardrobes, beds and dining tables. The prices are very reasonable and you buy the items on view at cash & carry prices (which include VAT), although delivery can be arranged. The oak furniture has a beautiful professional distressed finish – no veneers. All the timber used is from sustainable sources.

To complement your home – or someone else's if you are looking for presents, there is a wide range of decorative items including wood carvings, mirrors, chinaware, lamps, quilts, durries and cushions. In addition there is a large selection of framed prints of all sizes and types suitable for all tastes.

You can wander leisurely round either showroom and when totally spoilt for choice enjoy a free cup of tea or coffee whilst deciding which items to purchase. Remember to take your room sizes with you.

G.D. & Z. RUDKIN

Family firm devoted to traditional craftsmanship

The Old School, Station Road East, Grantham, Lincs NG31 6DH
☎ 0476 61477

St Pegas Granary, St Pegas Road, Peakirk, Peterborough PE6 7NF
☎ 0733 253465

Solid pine furniture, oak furniture, decorative items

Opening hours
Monday closed
Tuesday – Friday 11 – 7
Saturday 9 – 5
Sunday 11 – 4

Own car parks

Phoenix Hemming

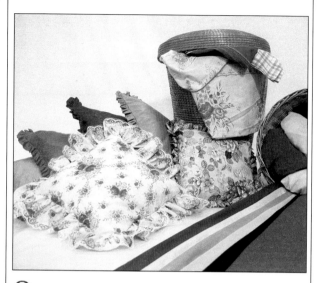

PHOENIX HEMMING

Unit 42, Alma Park Industrial Estate, Alma Park Road, Grantham, Lincs NG31 9SE

☎ 0476 590660

Bedding, duvets, lampshades, ready made curtains, cushions

Opening hours
Monday – Friday 10 – 4.30
Saturday 9 – 12.30

Free parking outside

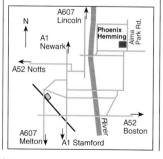

On the northern fringes of Grantham lies a small industrial estate and it is here that you will find the Phoenix Hemming factory. As the name suggests they 'hem' fabric into sheets, pillowcases, other bedding and curtains and cushions, the majority of which is used to fulfill orders from major department stores and hotels. However there is a small genuine factory shop at the front of building which sells a range of surplus products at very low prices.

Here you will find plain bedding in a range of colours and sometimes checked or patterned, most of it easy care. However they sometimes have 100% cotton, but suggest you telephone first to save yourself a journey.

90% of the products are made on the premises but quality duvets and velvet curtains are made elsewhere.

The shop is well organised but simple and you may have to wait a few minutes whilst the owner is called from the factory which can be viewed from an internal window. However a large size duvet cover from £8.75 is worth waiting for. There are plans afoot to widen the range of curtains available.

Hoops

10B Mill Street
Oakham
Rutland
Leicestershire
LE15 6EA

☎ 0572 756675

*Ladies designer & fashion
samples*

Opening hours
Monday – Saturday
9.30 – 5.30
Thursday 9.30 – 1.30

Street parking or free car
parks nearby

This Olde Worlde shop front in what was a row of stone cottages belies the modern interior. Inside you will find a large selection of good quality British and continental (mainly German) clothes. Many of the styles are what could be called modern classics in wonderful fabrics. Coats, jackets, skirts, trousers, dresses, blouses and knitwear are for sale at well below the normal retail price.

The keen prices are possible because they purchase manufacturers samples, 'end of ranges' and overmakes. All manufacturers make samples of designs before going into full production, sometimes they are left with them, and sometimes they make more than they have orders for; these are the garments that are on sale here. They are not 'seconds', but the prices are second to none. Sizes range from 10–20 (up to size 24 for suits, dresses and blouses) and the stock is constantly changing.

A variety of well-known fashion houses is represented, but if you have a particular favourite or require something for a special occasion please ask and they will do their best to meet your needs without putting you under obligation. They suggest frequent visits as the stock is constantly changing. You will find a welcome but no pressure.

Maltbys
COUNTRY STORE

Snell House
Brunel Drive
Newark
Nottinghamshire
NG24 2FB

☎ 0636 72591
Fax: 0636 71691

*Garden machinery,
horticultural supplies, DIY,
country clothing and toys*

Opening hours
Monday – Saturday 8 – 5

Ample free customer
parking

MALTBYS

This agricultural engineering business was founded in 1933 by Mr J.L. Maltby and still offers the same traditional personal service. However, in every other way it has moved with the times and expanded to offer a wide range of goods and services to all sections of the community. The purpose built modern building, occupying a 2 acre site, houses a wide range of garden machinery, horticultural supplies, tools and trailers, wellingtons and wheelbarrows. The D.I.Y. enthusiast will find a good selection of quality products from paint brushes to ladders.

The one-stop shopping concept is developing to include cookware, glassware and cleaning materials of all types – including small items such as plastic funnels and freezer boxes. Call in to browse and you are sure to find something you need – possibly even toys for the children!

They also stock a wide range of country clothing and safety clothing for those who have to brave the elements and other hazards. Expert advice is available for all products if required.

Their fully equipped service department will maintain or service your own machinery, collecting it and delivering it if you wish. The Stores department has over 20,000 different spare parts which can be traced in seconds by the computerised control system. A thoroughly modern traditional service.

MRS POTTERS PERFECT PORK

The Manor House,
Langford, Nr Newark
NG23 7RW

☎ 0636 611156

*Wide range of special meat
products, mainly pork,
especially sausages.*

In spite of the lovely photograph of lambs, Mrs Potter specialises in pork products, although lamb and beef are sometimes available of equally high quality.

An Old English pig, the Gloucester Old Spot forms the basis of the farm's herd of free range pigs. A great believer in 'happy pigs are healthy pigs', the emphasis is on humane husbandry. Living in family groups, the growing pigs are fed on natural foods. The combination of the breed of pig and humane methods answers many health and welfare concerns, Mr & Mrs Potter believe this greatly enhances the flavour, quality and texture of their products.

Their sausages containing a minimum of 80% meat, made to their own recipes, packed in natural hog casings are delicious.

The Manor House is a fine old building, set in parkland, and built for Bess of Hardwick's husband as a hunting lodge. At the side is the small modern well-equipped shop – open by appointment only please. Mrs Potters Perfect Pork can be found on Newark and Southwell markets. She also attends a number of major agricultural shows and horse trials.

Opening hours
Shop – Tuesdays and Thursdays 10 – 6
All other times by appointment

Newark Market, opp. Barclays Bank – Wednesdays & Fridays
Southwell Market – Saturday

NEWARK AIR MUSEUM

The Airfield
Winthorpe
Newark
Nottinghamshire
NG24 2NY

☎ 0636 707170

*Plastic aircraft kits, aviation
books and an extensive range
of aviation collectables*

Opening hours
Everyday except 24, 25, 26 Dec.
April – October
Weekdays 10 – 5
Weekends 10 – 6
November – March
Everyday 10 – 4

Ample free parking

The Newark Air Museum Shop is located on an aircraft dispersal point on the site of RAF Winthorpe, a former Second World War Bomber Base. It is believed the Museum Shop is the largest combined aircraft model and book shop in the region. Plastic kits stocked – Italeri; Heller; Monogram; Hasegawa; Matchbox; Revell; Fujimi; Airfix; Acadamy. Books published by – After the Battle; Ian Allen; PSL; Midland Counties; Osprey; Flypast; Aston and Airlife to name but a few.

As well as being "The Aviation Enthusiast's Dream" the Shop stocks an extensive range of aviation collectables which includes: Limited edition aviation art prints; Badges and pins; Posters; Postcards; Tea towels; Thimbles; Chinaware; Tapestries and Videos. Most items are now available on Mail Order. To receive lists and terms of trading telephone the museum or send in a large SAE.

Visit the museum itself which boasts a collection of more than 40 aircraft, or the nearby historic Market town of Newark-on-Trent. Remember there is no need to pay a museum admission fee if you just want to shop. Small children just starting to make models will be spoilt for choice and older, experienced modellers will find something new.

THE DRESS CIRCLE

The Dress Circle

16 Main Street
East Bridgford
Nottingham
NG13 8PA

☎ 0949 20861

*Ladies evening and cocktail
wear to hire or buy*

Opening hours
Monday 10 – 12
Wednesday 10 – 5
Thursday 10 – 7
Friday/Saturday 10 – 5

Road side parking

The small delightful village of East Bridgford is home to The Dress Circle, a most unlikely place to find a pretty double fronted shop specialising in beautiful evening wear. Designer evening dresses, gorgeous ballgowns and sensational cocktail dresses can be hired for a fraction of their real value. So why spend a fortune on one dress when you can have a different one for every special occasion? In sizes from 8 to 20, there's something for everyone, and the hire charges start at around £45. Most of the dresses can be altered to fit if required. The atmosphere is relaxed and informal and you are assured of unpressured personal attention. Complementary accessories are also stocked so clients can achieve the complete look for their special occasion. There is also a selection of dresses to purchase if preferred.

The business has grown considerably over the last five years and has recently moved into its present larger premises. Customers are drawn from a wide area thus re-inforcing The Dress Circle's reputation for only stocking quality garments in the latest designs. So next time you have a special occasion why not visit The Dress Circle?

Thaymar Dairy Ice Cream
Haughton Park Farm
Nr Bothamsall
DN22 8DB

☎ 0623 860320

Dairy Ice Cream
Farmshop
Tea room

Opening hours
Open daily 10 – 6
including Sundays
Closed Tuesday
Oct – March

Free parking outside

THAYMAR DAIRY ICE CREAM

Haughton Park Farm is a working dairy farm with a herd of Pedigree Friesians. The farm has been in the family since 1923, and is situated close to the pretty village of Bothamsall, in Notts., a few minutes from the A1. As farming practices have changed and diversification was needed, the family now produces quality Dairy Ice Cream using a traditional process and the finest natural ingredients; milk and double cream, raw cane sugar from Mauritius and natural flavourings from Italy.

The range of flavours is large and unusual – all of them delicious – and can be bought to eat there and then, or purchased in cartons for the freezer – remember to put your cool box in the car.

In addition to its well-known ice cream, the shop stocks Elizabeth King award-winning pork pies and sausages; jams, preserves and chutneys; fruit cordials, farm house biscuits, home made fresh cream gateaux, and other items – all carefully chosen for their quality.

The adjoining Cottage Tearoom offers homemade farmhouse fayre, morning coffee, cream teas, freshly made sandwiches, ploughman's lunches, and ice cream deserts – a good opportunity to 'taste' before you take a carton or two home?

GRANGE FARM POTTERY

Granby Lane, Plungar,
Nottingham NG13 0JJ

☎ 0949 60630

*Vases, plant hangers,
terracotta wall pots, kitchen
and tableware, house signs.*

Visitors are welcome at Grange Farm Pottery close to the canal in the small village of Plungar. It is easy to miss the sign so drive slowly, enjoy the scenery and turn into the farmyard. There you will find a converted barn housing the shop and workshop. Inside is a large selection of all types of pottery made on the premises and very reasonably priced for such high quality.

The majority of the pieces are dishwasher and microwave safe and all are ovenproof. They are mostly high fired stoneware using electric and gas fired kilns, and their distinctive hand-painted designs in subtle colours are achieved by using coloured slips (liquid clay) and coloured glazes. The range includes small practical kitchen items, storage jars, plates and casseroles and some large spectacular 'centre pieces' for gifts or special occasions. In addition there is a variety of terracotta wall pots and plant hangers and some large hand coiled garden pots – the latter are made elsewhere.

If you require something not on view please ask, as commissions are accepted by the highly skilled potter, who will cheerfully and helpfully discuss ways of meeting your particular specifications – a house sign for example!

Opening hours
Weekends 11 – 6
Weekdays by appointment,
please phone first

Parking in the yard

CUCHI INTERIORS

21–23 High Street,
Bassingham. Lincoln
LN5 9JZ

☎ 0522 788389

*Pine furniture, hand-carved
ornaments, Victorian style
bedding, picture gallery,
3–D dried flower pictures*

Opening hours
Tuesday 10 – 5
Friday 10 – 5
Saturday & Sunday 10 – 6

Parking outside

The village of Bassingham is midway between Lincoln and Newark on minor roads and a few miles from Stapleford Woods. Cuchi Interiors occupies a double fronted shop in the High Street – much larger than it appears having recently moved to obtain more space. It specialises in handcarved pine furniture sold at workshop prices. All their bed headboards are original designs from their own workshops and beautifully finished – matt antique, lacquered, limed or colour stained to your requirements. There is also a wide range of chests, wardrobes, dressing tables, tables, chairs and cupboards, and a selection of Victorian style bedding.

The picture gallery offers many original paintings and some beautifully framed prints at realistic prices. In addition Mrs Jones makes 3–D dried flower arrangements in frames and lampshades. The furniture showroom contains many unusual carved ornaments and small gift items at very reasonable prices.

If you are looking for special sizes in furniture, or a particular design, they will be happy to discuss your requirements and help if possible. Deliveries can be arranged over a wide area – just ask.

LOW WOODS FURNISHINGS

Low Woods Furnishings

Suppliers of Quality Fabrics

Low Woods, Belton,
Loughborough, Leics
LE12 9TR

☎ 0530 222246
FAX 0530 223932

*Soft furnishing fabrics,
accessories. Upholstery
fabrics, wallpapers*

Down a narrow country lane – drive carefully – you will find the entrance to Low Woods Furnishings, now housed in a converted barn after outgrowing its original stable.

Inside is a vast selection of curtain and upholstery fabrics. All are well-known brands and designer names such as Sanderson and Liberty, etc. It is unlikely that you will fail to find something to your taste, as the stock is always changing. Ends of rolls in short lengths are even better value.

You are free to browse. Should you need advice on measurements or styles, while a childrens television corner keeps your children amused, the staff are happy to help. Amongst the stock is a large selection of coloured lining, inter-lining, curtain accessories, trimmings, cord and ropes.

A wide range of upholstery fabric is always available. These range from linens, jacquards, damasks and natural undyed creams.

The family run business has an extensive making up service on the premises, backed by over 30 years experience.

They also sell top quality wall papers from stock, many more papers and fabrics from pattern books, and can order at discounted prices, although you may have to wait a few days for these.

Average price £7.00 per metre.

Opening hours
Monday closed
Tuesday – Saturday 9 – 5.30
Sunday 9 – 1

Own car park

17 Far Street, Wymeswold,
Loughborough, Leics
LE12 6TZ

☎ 0509 880309

Beautifully restored old pine.
Quality reproduction pine.
Locally produced craftwork.
Select cards.

Opening hours
Every day 9.30 – 5.30

Parking at side of building

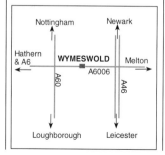

WYMESWOLD COUNTRY FURNITURE

These converted stables – sideways on to the road – once belonged to the old Manor House on the opposite side of the narrow entrance lane. Now they are gradually being renovated, but the old atmosphere remains. The business is expanding to house an ever widening selection of beautifully restored antique pine furniture. Each piece of furniture is personally selected by the owners and lovingly restored to its former glory. The stock includes wardrobes, chests, beds, desks, dressers, tables and numerous smaller and unusual items. Occasionally there are pieces of antique painted furniture, but these tend to sell very quickly as the prices are so reasonable.

The business has been established for 10 years, so is well-known locally. Some reproduction furniture is made on the premises and commissions undertaken if you have a specific requirement.

To compliment the furniture there is a selection of works by local crafts people, including some very attractive and unusual pottery, paintings and metal work, and some old pictures, household items, miniature chests and greetings cards.

Delivery of large items is free locally and further afield by arrangement, using the vintage delivery vehicle pictured above.

OLD DALBY LODGE FEEDS

Paddys Lane, Old Dalby,
Melton Mowbray, Leics
LE14 3LY

☎ 0509 880888

*Horse feeds, equestrian needs,
country clothing*

This business has grown over the years from selling horsefeeds such as Dodson & Horrell, and Dengie locally, to supplying everything from bridles and bedding to hoof picks and country clothing over a much wider area. Originally started by Mrs Morley it now occupies her husband also, while someone else runs the farm.

It is housed in an old tractor building which is larger than it appears, and holds a very large selection of countrywear including Musto fleeces and waterproofs – equally at home in town or country. Sherwood jackets are for children and adults, very attractive both in design and price. There are shooting jackets in Gortex fabric, Thermotex coats, country walking boots and leather paddock boots in addition to a wide large of jodhpurs and riding boots.

The range of horse accessories includes horse rugs and products from Cottage Craft, Hawkins, Aigle, Lavenham, Shires, B.H.B and Hydrophane. In fact everything for you and your horse can be obtained here, all at very reasonable prices.

The company also stocks a large trailer with merchandise to take to major horse events in the area and local point to points.

Opening hours
Monday – Saturday 9 – 6
Sunday 9 – 11.30

Own car park

35

NIPPERS – TUR LANGTON

The Manor, Tur Langton,
Leicester LE8 0PJ

☎ 0858 545434

*New and second-hand baby
equipment, indoor and
outdoor toys.*

Opening hours
Monday, Tuesday,
Wednesday and Friday
9.30 – 4.30
Thursday 9.30 – 7
Saturday 9.30 – 5
Sunday 2 – 4.30

Parking in farmyard

The winding road between Melton Mowbray and Market Harborough passes through the small attractive village of Tur Langton and here you will find 'The Manor', which has a barnful of surprises! The photograph above shows only part of the large display of baby equipment and toys for sale at very reasonable prices.

Inside you will find a happy friendly atmosphere and a huge collection of prams from Mon Bébé, Albion, Bébé Confort and Britax. Upstairs are adjustable cots of all types, play-pens, high chairs, bouncers and baby walkers, plus bedding and safety equipment. In short, all the equipment needed to make life easier with small children. Some of the items are 'seconds', and consequently even cheaper than normal, but the flaws are slight – probably a scratch that the average family would produce in a very short time anyway. There is also a range of good quality second-hand equipment.

Toys by Fisher Price, Little Tikes and Brio amongst others are bright, colourful and educational. At the rear of the premises is a totally enclosed display and demonstration area for outdoor toys.

If you are taking children with you they will be entranced by the small animals on view at the farm. A tea shop is planned also.

HOMEBIRDS

Langton Hall stands in beautiful rolling countryside with a sweeping driveway to the hall and coach house. The latter is a light spacious building filled with thousands of metres of top quality soft furnishing fabrics at most reasonable prices. The selection of 'seconds' and perfect quality is vast and constantly changing – chosen from the top designer names. You will find everything from the lightest silks to the heaviest upholstery fabrics, although the largest range consists of various weights of curtaining fabrics. Elegant stripes, modern and traditional weaves and designs, chintz – plain and patterned, and varied checks abound – you will be quite spoiled for choice.

The business has existed for five years, and partners Pauline Kirby and Bridget Bibby have built up a large clientele not only because of the incredible range of fabrics, but because of the personal attention given to their clients. Their stock includes all the accessories required such as linings, tapes and hooks but if you prefer they offer a full making-up service including loose covers and re-upholstery.

In addition there are some lovely pieces of old furniture, dried flower arrangements, cushions, rugs and wallpapers to enhance your home. A real treasure trove!

HALSTEAD & FOWLER
CABINET MAKERS

Blythe House
4 Park Road
Holbeach
Nr. Spalding
Lincs PE12 7EE

☎ 0406 425173

*Reproduction period furniture
1 offs & commissions
Upholstery & materials
Restoration*

Opening hours
Monday – Friday 8 – 5.30
Saturday 8 – 5

Free parking outside

HALSTEAD & FOWLER

When you have a favourite piece of furniture, you very often want to have it matched with other pieces, have it repaired if it is damaged, or re-upholstered or french polished to update it. The firm of Halstead & Fowler at Holbeach are cabinet makers and joiners of the highest standard, well known throughout the Eastern countries for their high quality work.

There are three aspects to their services. First, they specialise in making one-off and commissioned pieces of period furniture to your own design (they offer a design service) and specifications. Traditional cabinet making practices are used with solid timber, man-made boards, decorative veneers and inlays. The piece can then be stained and polished to match your requirements. Secondly, a complete upholstery service is offered for both antique and modern furniture, with a large range of traditional and modern fabrics and braids to choose from.

Upholstery materials e.g. foam, webbing, needles are also sold. Thirdly, a polishing service is offered, with traditional french polish and wax finish for antique furniture, and sprayed lacquers for modern. Repairs of all kinds can be undertaken, in fact joinery of any kind that cannot be bought off the shelf. In effect, a high quality firm offering high quality work at reasonable rates.

THE NATIONAL TRUST IN NORFOLK

BLICKLING HALL

The National Trust administers in Norfolk the nationally known country houses of Blickling Hall, near Aylsham, Felbrigg Hall, near Cromer, and Oxburgh Hall, near King's Lynn.

There are interesting gift shops at all three, all of which are open April–October with the Hall & Gardens (normally four or five days each week, in the afternoons). In addition, the shops also open in November and December for Christmas Shopping. Blickling and Felbrigg have restricted opening hours from January to March which also covers the January Sale. (Individual opening times are listed at the side of the page). In stock is a wide range of quality products including china, books, toys, trays, jams and preserves, confectionery and craft products. Many of the latter are made locally.

Blickling Hall and Felbrigg Hall are 17th Century houses with great collections, beautiful gardens, and are surrounded by magnificent woods and parkland. Oxburgh Hall is a late 15th Century moated house with a colourful French parterre and woodland walks.

All these beautiful houses offer you the opportunity of combining lovely walks in the open air with your shopping for interesting gifts. The shops can be visited without paying admission charges and all have restaurants and free parking.

BLICKLING HALL
Blickling, Nr. Aylsham, Norwich
☎ 0263 733084

Open
Hall, Garden & Shop –
April–Oct. – Tues, Wed, Fri, Sat, Sun, B.Hol.Mon. 1–5
Shop & Garden open 11.00
Shop only – *Nov & Dec* – Thurs–Sun 11–4
Jan–Mar – Sat & Sun 11–4

FELBRIGG HALL
Felbrigg, Nr. Cromer
☎ 0263 837444

Open
Hall, Garden & Shop –
April–Oct. – Mon, Wed, Thurs, Sat, Sun 1–5
(Shop opens 12, Garden 11)
Shop only – *Nov & Dec* – Thurs–Sun 11–4
Jan–Mar – Sat & Sun 11–4

OXBURGH HALL
Oxborough, King's Lynn
☎ 0366 328258

Open
Hall, Garden & Shop –
April–Oct. – Sat–Wed 1–5
(Garden opens 12)
Shop only – *Nov & Dec* – Sat & Sun 11–4

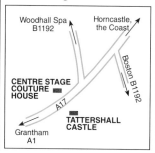

CENTRE STAGE COUTURE HOUSE

Couture House

Bridge House, Sleaford Road, Tattershall, Lincs LN4 4LR

☎ 0526 342849

Made to measure and off the peg daywear, wedding gowns, cocktail and evening wear . Available in stock or custom made to match an outfit, designer jewellery, shoes, handbags, bridal headresses, veils cut to size, hats blocked and trimmed and wedding flowers.

Opening hours
Open throughout the year, evenings and weekends by appointment. Shop opening summer 1994 when no appointment will be needed.

Parking to the door

Centre Stage specialise in creating the total look for the bride, with perfectly coordinated garments, hats, head dresses, veils, shoes, handbags, jewellery and even flowers. The studios are situated in picturesque Georgian gardens, opposite Tattershall Castle, a relaxing atmosphere for choosing special clothes and accessories. Bridal and evening collections are available ready to wear, also day wear and business wear. However all garments may be created specially for clients, a very valuable service for the bride and her mother, where colour coordination is important across many accessories. Design sessions are by appointment. All accessories can be created especially for the outfit. The Centre Stage Couture artiste has attended to, and created for, The Royal Family, and worked with many famous London Couture Houses.

The studio and shop are filled with colourful and stylish garments and materials collected from all over the world to ensure totally stunning outfits.

Centre Stage work very similarly to the well-loved BBC House of Elliot creating clothes that are of the quality and style perfect for the person and the occasion, although they will also work to the individual client's budget – there is a hire service for bridal and evening wear if required. A visit to this studio is an experience in itself.

HOLKHAM HALL POTTERY AND GIFT SHOPS

Holkham Estate Office
Wells–Next–The–Sea
Norfolk
NR23 1AB

☎ 0328 710227

Holkham Pottery, established in 1951, produces a wide and attractive range of flower vases, lamps, tableware and ornamental gifts. The two shops also stock a huge range of original items which not only make ideal presents, but happen to be useful as well!

The shops are located in the ancient house on the A149 coast road in Holkham village – almost opposite Lady Ann's Road to the beach – and adjacent to Holkham Hall itself.

Holkham Hall is situated in a 3,000 acre deer park with magnificent trees and a lake. It is a classic 18th century Palladian style mansion with a magnificent marble entrance hall, and still part of a great agricultural estate.

Opening times
At the Ancient House:
Open daily from Good Friday unti the end of October; weekends only in November and December, plus special Christmas opening days (phone for details: 0328 710424).
All 10 – 5
(closed for lunch 1 – 2)

At Holkham Hall:
Easter, May, Spring & Summer Bank Holiday Sundays and Mondays; End May to end September, Sunday to Friday inc. October, Monday to Friday inc. All 10–5

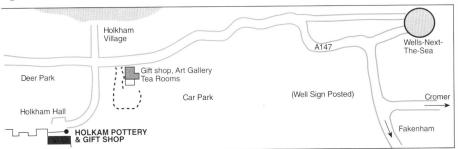

Cressy Hall, Gosberton,
Spalding, Lincs PE11 4JD

☎ 0775 840925

*Cast iron garden furniture
& urns*

Opening hours
Monday – Friday 10 – 4
Other times please phone
for appointment

Parking on premises

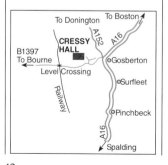

MICHAEL HILL

If you really appreciate beautiful things and love your garden you cannot fail to be impressed by this furniture. It is genuine cast iron, exact copies of antique designs, which are shown off to perfection in the garden of a stately Georgian hall tucked away down a long narrow lane in the Fens.

The enduring qualities of cast iron make it the ideal material for garden furniture. The strength of the metal, however, does not detract from the lightness and delicacy achieved in these intricate copies of the most fashionable Victorian designs. Exact replicas are painstakingly cast in sand, in the age-old way, then each piece is fine-fettled, carefully assembled and painted by hand in the workshops at Cressy Hall.

Prices for a bench seat start at £399 which is considerably lower than the genuine antique, and of course, in far superior condition. The range includes chairs, benches, tables, love seat, urns and fountains.

The chairs and benches are both attractive in look and practical in use and would enhance a conservatory or formal terrace and be equally delightful in a wild woodland glade or shady arbour.

THE PINE WORKSHOPPE

School House, Scoulton,
Norwich NR9 4NY

☎ 0953 851338

*Pine furniture, oak furniture,
decorative items*

Opening hours
Monday-Saturday 10 – 5
Sun & Bank Holidays 11 – 4

Own car park

The old schoolhouse has been completely renovated inside, and extended to provide interesting showrooms of nearly 5,000 sq. feet. The products are shown to advantage in this setting and consist of traditionally made reproduction solid pine furniture, all hand finished and good quality. Furniture can be found here to suit all rooms in the house, whether you require a large dresser or small bedside cabinet. Many purchasers start with a few pieces and add to their collection over a period of time, knowing that the style will match. Some furniture is made from re-claimed old timber and some pieces are genuine antiques. The friendly assistants are knowledgeable and helpful, and there, if required.

One room is devoted to oak reproduction furniture, with a lovely finish. Although the range on show is small, other pieces can be ordered specially.

The showrooms are decorated with interesting small items, also for sale, consisting of wrought-iron candlesticks, lamps and pictures or pottery, and what the owner, Gina Duggan, describes as 'kitchenalia'. No home is complete without its 'bits & pieces'.

Delivery of large items is free over a wide area and by arrangement elsewhere. Well worth a visit.

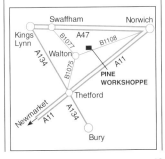

Fieldstead Farm,
off New Road, Impington,
Cambridge

☎ 0223 237799

*Fruit, vegetables, preserves,
home baked cakes and pies,
frozen pre-pacekd meals*

Opening hours
*June, July, August (Summer
openings)*
Monday – Friday 9 – 7
Saturday & Sunday 9 – 6
Rest of year 7 days 9 – 6

Own car park

CHIVERS FARM SHOP

This business has come a long way since it started as a 'Pick your own' shop. Now it sells practically everything one expects from a quality grocers and greengrocers. Everything on sale has been specially selected for quality or grown on the adjoining fruit farm. The range of fruit includes strawberries, raspberries, blackberries, black and red currants, and gooseberries which are 'pick your own' in season or sold 'blast' frozen in cartons out of season. Apples and pears are also farm grown.

Jams, marmalades, chutneys, fudge and apple juice are their 'own label'. Cake and pies are home produced and sell out quickly. Fresh vegetables, fresh soups and fresh pastas are available and a good selection of smoked meat and fish. In fact the list of good quality products is endless and even includes fruit trees and plants if you prefer to grow your own. The family pet is catered for with a variety of pet foods and snacks.

The shop is well organised and self-service – I must mention the delightful willow shopping baskets – although very friendly and knowledgeable staff are at hand if needed, which ensures a pleasant relaxed atmosphere.

A tea room is planned for early 1995 which will make a visit here even more enjoyable. Remember to put the cool-box in the car!

NURSERY DAYS

Nursery · Days ·

Home Farm, Graveley,
Huntingdon, Cambs
PE18 9PL

☎ 0480 830841
Fax: 0480 830641

*Nursery & Baby equipment
including Silver Cross,
Mamas & Papas, Cosatto,
Maclaren, Tomy, Fisher Price,
Playskool.*

Opening hours
Monday closed
Tuesday, Wednesday,
Friday 10 – 4.30
Thursday 2 – 8,
Saturday 9 – 5

Ample free parking

A former stable block has been converted to a large attractive shop stocking everything parents need for a new arrival. It is run by sisters Susan Langstaff and Louise Wilson, who are themselves parents of young children, so they fully understand the needs of parents and have stocked the shop accordingly. You can choose from a range of 30 different styles of prams, one of the largest selections in the county, including Silver Cross, Mamas & Papas and Swallow to name but a few. A deposit will secure any item until needed and all prices are very competitive. In addition they stock playpens, car seats, high chairs, cots and carrycots, bedding and safety equipment.

You are welcome to browse at leisure and to try the equipment in your own car for size and convenience. You will be spoilt for choice. The ages catered for are birth to nursery age. Small children are delighted to find a range of Fisher-Price and Playskool toys on sale and grandparents are known to be equally delighted.

The atmosphere is friendly, helpful and relaxed and only 10 minutes drive off the main roads into a pretty village which also boasts a good village pub.

There is ample free parking, and toilet and baby-changing facilites – a delightful place to shop.

WIMPOLE HALL
Royston, Herts
☎ 0223 207257

Open – *April – October*
Tues, Wed, Thurs, Sat, Sun,
B.Hol. 10.30–5.30
(Hall open 1.00–5.00)
Nov–March – (Hall not open)
Tues, Wed, Thurs, Sat & Sun 11–4
Free admission to shop

ANGLESEY ABBEY
Lode, Cambridge
☎ 02233 811200

Open – *April – October*
April–Mid-July
Wed–Sun, B.Hol. 11–5.30
Mid-July–Early Sept.
Daily 11–5.30
House open 1–5. Garden from 11.
Nov & Dec – Thurs–Sun 11–4
Jan–Mar – Sat & Sun 11–4
House not open.
Free admission to shop

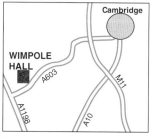

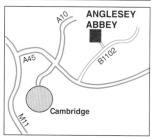

THE NATIONAL TRUST IN CAMBRIDGESHIRE

WIMPOLE HALL

Most of us do not associate the names of great ancient houses like Wimpole Hall and Anglesey Abbey, both near the glorious University City of Cambridge, with shopping, but both these lovely houses can provide you with interesting shopping in beautiful surroundings. Why not enjoy a magnificent 100 acre garden and shop at the same time?

Wimpole Hall, 8 miles S.W. of Cambridge on the A603 (off the M11), is an 18th century house set in a superb landscaped park. There is also a Rare Breeds Farm. The shop is located in a Victorian Stable Block which also houses a light refreshments area and a Saddlery. The shop offers craft goods, books, china, toys, confectionery, preserves. You will delight in the gardens as Queen Victoria did in 1843.

Anglesey Abbey, 6 miles N.E. of Cambridge on the B1102 (off the A45), is famous today for its magnificent 100 acre garden, particularly the Hyacinth Garden, a fantasy of colour. Most remarkable is the fascinating collection of Statuary and the interesting Lode Mill, still working, tucked away in the north of the garden. The shop is located in the Visitor Centre, with a range of products including china, books, toys, craft products, confectionery and preserves. The Plant Centre has a wide and interesting range of plants for sale.

WOOD GREEN ANIMAL SHELTERS

You may be surprised to find this fascinating place included in the guide but it is one of the most popular venues in East Anglia. Many people travel great distances so the facilities available ensure your visit is enjoyable, interesting and educational. Primarily a home for unwanted animals, from hamsters to llamas, visitors are welcome to walk round the 50-acre site and see for themselves the care and attention given. If you are looking for a family pet your enquiries are welcome and help is at hand.

The nature of the work carried out here requires large sums of money, hence a variety of money raising events such as exhibitions, craft fairs, equestrian events and other forms of entertainment take place in the Britten Arena, which was specially built to international standards, for Riding and Driving for the Disabled.

The large shop has an extensive range of pet food and accessories at competitive prices. In addition there is a good selection of own logo pottery and kitchen items, plus jewellery, books, and cruelty free cosmetics. In short there is something for everyone. The normal shop profits are covenanted to the shelters to enable their good work to continue. Your visit can be rounded off in the Kings Bush Restaurant with a coffee or a full banquet.

Two other locations at Heydon and Wood Green

THE CURTAIN EXCHANGE

This is one of a small chain of shops throughout the country selling second-hand curtains on a commission basis in much the same way as a dress agency operates. Top quality curtains are hung around the walls of the four rooms 'where extravagant swags of fabric contrive the happy atmosphere of a Middle Eastern bazaar' according to the Daily Telegraph Weekend (Eric Bailey) July 27th 1991. However, you will not need to haggle over the prices as they usually average about one-third of the original price.

All curtains are inspected for condition before being accepted and many of them have never been hung. Some are straight from manufacturers with cancelled orders, some from showhouses, interior designers or window displays. Many are there simply because the original owner decided against them when seeing them in the home setting. If you are looking for quality curtains to tone in with a particular colour scheme take your window measurements and room size with you, plus carpet and wallpaper samples.

The range is constantly changing and includes small cotton curtains and elegant ballroom ones. An alteration service is offered, and should you prefer fabric off the roll (available in limited quantities) a making-up service is offered.

You may also find cushions, bedspreads and home accessories.

EISKE COATS

Crows Hall, Debenham,
Suffolk IP14 6NG

☎ 0728 860246

*Waterproof coats, two weights
of lining*

You may have seen these marvellous coats at agricultural shows and wondered where they were made or where else you could purchase one.

They are made in an Elizabethan moated manor house deep in the Suffolk countryside, but please only visit by telephoning first for an appointment, prices start at £134.

The Eiske collection offers a range of high quality waterproof coats, which are very warm, very light, and wind proof, but of a breathable material which avoids perspiration. They are ideal for the woman who demands a combination of comfort, practicality and modern British styling – colourful yet tastefully refined. They are available with two different weights of fleece lining. The first is warm and suitable for most conditions, and the heavier one is ideal for those who especially feel the cold. These versatile garments are ideal for all outdoor activities and so roomy and light that they are comfortable to drive in.

Each Eiske coat is made with fabric proofed with the 'Milair' process which is your guarantee of quality, long life and hand washability of your coat. Send for a brochure or see them in the Rural Crafts Association marquee at agricultural shows.

Opening hours
Telephone for appointment. Can also be seen at Suffolk Show, Royal Norfolk Show, Burghley Horse Trails and Crafts for Christmas Suffolk

Parking outside

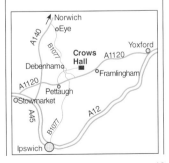

NIPPERS – WHITE COLNE

White's Farm, Bures Road,
White Colne, Colchester
CO6 2QF

☎ 0787 228000

*New and second-hand baby
equipment, indoor and
outdoor toys.*

Opening hours
Tuesday 10 – 4
Thursday 2 – 6 (&
6 – 8 by appointment)
Friday 10 – 4
Saturday 9.30 – 5

Own car park

This large barn in the beautiful countryside of the Essex/Suffolk border seems an unlikely place to go for nursery equipment and toys, but you will find a warm welcome, ample free parking and an incredibly large selection. Partners Catherine Winser and Sally Scobie have young children themselves so are fully aware of everything required to satisfy your needs. They have a large stock of new, 'seconds', and second-hand prams, cots, play-pens and high chairs by leading manufacturers, and bedding.

The range of toys includes Fisher Price, Brio, and Little Tikes. Small children are in their element trying them out whilst their parents look at larger items or fit child seats into their cars.

The shop area is well laid out and everything is clearly marked with prices, which are very reasonable, if you prefer only to browse. Large items can be stored until required. Also in stock are devices to make your home safer for small children, such as stairgates and baby alarms.

The atmosphere is friendly and relaxed but totally professional. Toilet and baby changing facilities are available.

SNAPE MALTINGS

SNAPE MALTINGS
RIVERSIDE CENTRE

Snape, Nr. Saxmundham,
Suffolk IP17 1SR

☎ 0728 688305

*House & garden shop
Craft shop, countrywear,
paintings, books and toys,
classical CD's and cassettes*

Opening hours
Every day all year
(except Dec 25 & 26)
Summer 10 – 6
Winter 10 – 5

Free parking

The famous Snape Maltings near Aldeburgh is a genuine surprise. This attractive collection of mellow red-brick malthouses and granaries houses a fascinating collection of shops and galleries, a tea shop – and even a pub!

The House & Garden shop offers a wide range of products for the house – rugs and quilts, kitchenware, furniture and decorative items, as well as herbs and plants. The fine foods, pickles and preserves are most attractive. The Snape Craft Shop presents a selection of finely crafted gifts, many by East Anglian craftsmen. Countrywear offers practical country clothing, including a stylish range of sweaters. The Books and Toys centre is especially attractive to children, but also offers books, cards and stationery for older visitors. Classical CDs, particularly the works of Benjamin Britten and other Snape concert recordings are available at Maltings Music. For original paintings and limited edition prints, the Gallery is the area to be looked into. An unusual feature is the Christmas Shop, open from September to Christmas with a wide range of festive season decorations.

Why is shopping at the Snape a real alternative? Stand on the banks of the timeless River Alde and look out across the quiet, endless East Anglian shore, and you will realize you have bought more than just goods.

VANNERS *Silk Weavers*

Gregory Street, Sudbury,
Suffolk

☎ 0787 313933

*Silk by the metre, many
unusual silk gifts*

Opening hours
Monday – Friday 9 – 5
Saturday 9 – 12
Xmas – New Year closed.
Additional hours at sale
time.

Own free car park opposite

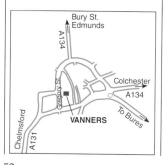

VANNERS SILK – MILL SHOP

As one of the oldest companies still weaving silk fabrics in England, Vanners Silk has a pedigree stretching back to circa 1730 when it was part of the Spitalfields silk industry in London. The move to Sudbury took place in the mid 19th century.

Today Vanners specialises in producing woven silk fabric for clients all over the world, using only the finest craftsmanship and the best silks available to weave fine intricate designs. As you enter the shop the looms in the factory can be seen through an interior window. They are one of the few companies that still process silk from its raw state to the woven fabric.

The shop has an abundance of silk by the metre in weights and designs suitable for blouses, dresses, dressing gowns and nightwear. You will also find some beautiful and unusual small items, such as purses, wallets, card cases and spectacle cases in silk and leather at about half the expected price. The range of silk ties, cravats, waistcoats and dressing gowns for gentlemen should appeal to all tastes. The range of silk squares covers all sizes and tastes and there is even some silk jewellery in glowing colours and silk embroidered greetings cards – irresistible!

STUDIO CERAMICS

Studio Ceramics

72 Fosse Road
Farndon
Newark

☎ 0636 73527
Fax 0636 612871

*Floor and wall tiles in
Ceramic, Terracotta and Slate*

Opening hours
Monday – Friday 9 – 5.30
Saturday 9 – 4

Free parking outside

Studio Ceramics Limited are conveniently situated on the outskirts of Newark adjacent to the A46 and Newark by-pass at Farndon. Their show rooms contain an extensive range of exclusive European ceramic, terracotta and slate tiles for floors and walls. A wonderful variety of designs, most of which are available immediately from their separate stock warehouse. Bulk buying by the company enable Studio Ceramics to supply tiles of high quality at very competitive prices for kitchens, bathrooms and conservatories.

The company is renowned for its friendliness, personal service and planning expertise. If you wish they also provide a quality installation service. For those who prefer to tackle the job themselves a tile cutter can be hired and fixing materials purchased.

Whilst the showroom is situated on the main road the village of Farndon is actually on the River Trent, with a large Marina and boatyard, The Lazy Otter riverside pub and extensive riverside walks. So why not round off your shopping down by the river, a two minute drive away.

BRIDGE COTTAGE
Flatford, Nr East Bergholt,
Nr Colchester, Essex
☎ 0206 298260

Open
April–Oct. – Wed–Sun & B. Hol.
Mon 11–5.30,
Daily 10–5.30 *June–Sept*
Nov – Wed–Sun 11–3.30
Free admission to shop

GUILDHALL OF CORPUS CHRISTI
Market Place, Lavenham
☎ 0787 247646

Open
April–Oct. – Daily 11–5
(closed Good Friday)
Free admission to shop

ICKWORTH HOUSE
The Rotunda, Horringer,
Bury St. Edmunds
Tel. 0284 735270

Open
April–Oct. – Tues, Wed, Fri, Sat,
Sun & B. Hol. Mon 1.30–5.30
Garden & Park Open all year
Shop – Open as house +
Nov & Dec Sat & Sun 11–4
Admission to shop with park &
Garden ticket

THE NATIONAL TRUST IN SUFFOLK

ICKWORTH

You may not have on your shopping list a Constable painting, but you can combine viewing his masterpeices with your shopping at the National Trust! Bridge Cottage at Flatford near Flatford Mill.

Shops selling products as varied as china, toys, preserves, craft products, prints and books are also open at Ickworth House at Horringer, near Bury St. Edmunds and at the Guildhall of Corpus Christi at Lavenham.

The fascinating Guildhall of Corpus Christi is an early 16th Century timber-framed building in Lavenham's market place, housing exhibitions on the local woollen industry, farming and railways, and has a delightful Walled Garden. Ickworth is one of the most extraordinary great houses in England, with superb collections of silver and paintings, and is again surrounded by extensive gardens and a beautiful park and deer enclosure. The Constable exhibition in Bridge Cottage even has guided tours from the cottage to the sites of his paintings. All three have catering facilities, and at Ickworth there is a children's play area.

It adds so much to the pleasure of shopping when you can enjoy such gentle and beautiful surroundings at the same time.

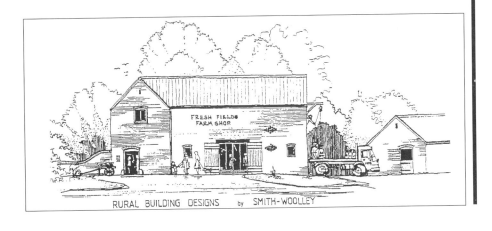

INDEX
LOCATION AND PRODUCTS

INDEX
ALPHABETICAL

For details of what is sold please refer to the map location index page.

Further copies of this book may be obtained directly from the publishers at £3.25 (to include postage and packing).

Please make your cheque payable to *The Stable Publishing Company* (no order will be accepted without prior payment). and post to:

> The Stable Publishing Company
> Woolsthorpe by Belvoir
> Grantham
> Lincolnshire
> NG32 1NT

Books in this series due out shortly:

> The Alternative Shopping Guide to
> Cheshire, North Wales, Staffordshire & North
> Shropshire
>
> The Alternative Shopping Guide to
> The South East
>
> *Other areas are in the course of preparation.*

This page has been left blank for your own notes.